Innocence

poems by

Patricia Carragon

Finishing Line Press
Georgetown, Kentucky

Innocence

*A special thanks to Amy Barone, Brenda J. Gannam,
Davidson Garrett, Cindy Hochman, Susan H. Maurer,
and Karen Neuberg.
Your friendship and support gave me the courage to persevere.*

Copyright © 2017 by Patricia Carragon
ISBN 978-1-63534-152-2 First Edition
All rights reserved under International and Pan-American Copyright Conventions.
No part of this book may be reproduced in any manner whatsoever without written permission from the publisher, except in the case of brief quotations embodied in critical articles and reviews.

ACKNOWLEDGMENTS

"Innocence." First published in *The Best of Stain Anthology*, Vol. 1, Winter '08-'09.
"Dandelion Child." First published in *Tamarind*, March 2008.
"The Green Crayon." *Postcard Poems and Prose Magazine*, January 20, 2014.
"Picture of Life." First published in *The Culvert Chronicles*, July 16-22, 2009.
"Chandelier." *Inertia*, 2010.
"The Palace." First published in *Luciole Press*, March 2008.
"Humoresque." From "Journey to the Center of My Mind," *Rogue Scholars Press*, 2005.
"Dead Flower." From "Journey to the Center of My Mind," *Rogue Scholars Press*, 2005.
"Subterranean Passage." *Chanterelle's Notebook* Issue #13, August 2008.
"Bird Watch." First published in *The Toronto Quarterly*, Issue 1, 2008.
Continued on Page 32

Publisher: Leah Maines

Editor: Christen Kincaid

Cover Art: Bob Heman

Author Photo: Patricia Carragon

Cover Design: Elizabeth Maines

Printed in the USA on acid-free paper.
Order online: www.finishinglinepress.com
also available on amazon.com

Author inquiries and mail orders:
Finishing Line Press
P. O. Box 1626
Georgetown, Kentucky 40324
U. S. A.

Table of Contents

Innocence	1
Dandelion Child	2
The Green Crayon	3
Picture of Life	4
Chandelier	5
The Palace	6
Humoresque	8
Dead Flower	10
Subterranean Passage	11
Bird Watch	12
Network	13
Frozen Kisses	14
Coming Home	15
Open Space	16
The Shabbat Eve	17
An Ordinary Girl	18
The Ghost	20
When I Die	21
Small Dreams	22
Scheduled Departures	23
The Room	24
Unchaperoned	25
Mr. Lipson	26
Roller Coaster Train	29
The 4-Dimensional Man	30

Innocence

Innocence came out to play
and saw storm clouds instead.

The fluffy days of childhood
played tag with problems,
but never could get the stains out
as new problems settled in.

We still wash our dirty laundry
not expecting them to look
squeaky clean.

The more we scrub,
the darker the stains
after each rinse.

We dry our clothes inside,
never hang our history
on a clothesline.

It would only clash against
the pretty greenery
next door
and the neighbors
would complain.

Dandelion Child

An umbrella spins
like a kaleidoscope.
A child plays tag with it—
raindrops tease her skin.
Her smile defies the weather.

She scoots across
with arms raised against etiquette.
The umbrella dances
under rain-washed sky.
The child is like a dandelion—
her seeds bounce
like raindrops.

Her sister joins in—
the umbrella lands upside down.
Her sister hides
behind the azalea bush.
They forget about
their wet clothes
and hair,
dinner,
and the umbrella.

Their mother watches
from the kitchen window
and is not amused.
She taps on the glass
for the girls to come inside.
Her persistence synchronizes
with the thunder.
Then the game ends
as raindrops beat down
on her daughters' heads.
The kitchen door slams
and lightning breaks
into a hundred forks.

The Green Crayon

The green crayon lit her imagination. Like a cigarette, it dangled from her mouth. But the girl accidentally swallowed it and thought she was going to die. Her parents said that she wouldn't. She changed her mind after a trip to the bathroom. She learned to draw shortly after.

The girl's crayons processed magic, especially the green one. She drew flowers and animals everywhere—walls and furniture were included. When she attended kindergarten, the magic fizzled. Scribble-scrabble was no longer an art form—her imagination learned to stay within the lines. As she initialed her first project, the green crayon's point snapped. Her imagination immediately left the classroom.

Picture of Life

A painting's still in progress—
Parisian life
numbered for color.
People sit at an outdoor café,
sip wine
between conversations.
A man delivers his wares
in an ancient
but sturdy wagon
as long as his horse
can be of service.

But the artist
didn't finish her piece.
Instead,
she allowed age
to paint the edges,
kept some areas
devoid of color.
Inside her dented box,
capsules have lost their oil.
Brushes lie unwashed,
too brittle for use—
inertia lives in the dust.
I wonder why,
but the artist isn't here
to answer.

Chandelier

hanging from
a brass chain
the electrified
octopus
dressed in crystal
turned into
a chandelier

hanging from
a brass chain
the spider
had a similar idea
but the chain
turned into
a noose

The Palace

The palace became a wreck in seconds—
a child was caught in between the bricks,
but he left the scene with minor injuries.
Yet the palace was not destroyed,
nor was the child hurt.
In fact, there was no palace or child present—
the palace was never built
since there were no blueprints.
There were no architects summoned
to conceive the idea to build it.
The child was never born
since there was no conception.
There was no love to build a family
that would include him—
imagination wrote this story
to disturb my mind.

Yet I read about it in a newspaper today:
the palace became a wreck in seconds—
a child was caught in between the bricks,
but he left the scene with minor injuries—
but some people say
that the palace was not destroyed,
nor was the child hurt.
In fact, they say
that the palace was never built
since there were no blueprints
or architects summoned
to conceive the idea to build it
and the child was never born
since there was no conception
or love to build a family
that would include him.

Yet the palace did become a wreck in seconds
and a child did get caught in between the bricks,
and he did leave the scene with minor injuries—
and so it was, according to the newspaper
and my mind.

But the palace was not destroyed,
nor was the child hurt.
In fact, there was no palace or child present—
the palace was never built
since there were no blueprints.
There were no architects summoned
to conceive the idea to build it.
The child was never born
since there was no conception.
There was no love to build a family
that would include him—
imagination wrote this story
to disturb me during sleep.

I woke up and turned on the television.

A house near Beirut became a wreck in seconds—
a child was caught in between the bricks
and was crushed to death . . .

Humoresque

The ringmaster steps forward,
identifies me in the darkness.
I'm a criminal caught by fate,
tried by limelight.
The circle enlarges,
delights a jury of fools,
bedazzles the impatience
shouting in the bleachers.

People are starving for comic relief;
the heat of lupine drama roars—
the show begins . . .
I juggle scenes from my life.
Clowns see underneath make-up,
snatch my face,
strip my psyche.
They laugh,
pull my hair,
toss water in my face—
bread and circus
feeds the hungry mimes of prey.

The final act serves its tart dessert
as clowns beat me with props.
My pasty skin is no different than
the polka dots on their costumes,
but the crowd demands more.
Clowns acquiesce,
attach leeches to my psyche.
The crowd cheers . . .
Blood seals my name—
an aperitif to quench their thirst
paid in revenge.

Behind a torn curtain,
you watch in horror.
Sacred appellation
bleeds from my eyes.
Your imagination pulls me
away from the noose.
On a stolen mare,
we jump through the fiery ring,
escape from the roar
of the human stampede.

Dead Flower

I may be fluent in maturity,
but I'm still a child
who walks awkwardly in high heels.
In adult clothes,
I speak adult words,
pretend to be grown up.
Yet I'm still a child,
who holds a dead flower
and hides behind adult clothes
and words,
fearing that at any moment,
someone might expose
the shame of a fairytale princess
who forgot how to cry.

Subterranean Passage

A woman in a hurry
falls out of step
between her schedule
and a distraction
on the subway stairs.
A scruffy hipster passes—
his savoir-flair startles her.
Her eyes turn towards him,
but the wind interferes.
Her long red hair
hides her face.
Serendipitous patterns
can't turn his eyes away
from the wall's nondescript
geometry.
Before she could sketch
a conversation,
he was gone.
All possibilities drawn
for a match or mistake
were quietly erased
by the wind.

Bird Watch

competitive nests hum after 8 p.m.—
feathered creatures flock to bars
along second avenue.

peacocks in suits
clink beer bottles,
sing karaoke off-key.

peafowl in raised hemlines
play sexual pantomime.

robins and canaries
wing it with penguin bartenders,
and flamingos sashay
to the disco beat.

the night brings them in—
those sugar daddy owls,
fast-talking hummingbirds,
and gossipmonger parrots.

pigeons outnumber the exotics,
and too many chickens and turkeys
make the scene foul.

in the corner,
a sparrow sips her merlot,
thinks about scrambled eggs
and flying solo.

the wine gives her courage,
but her wings are too stiff
to make the move.

Network

I'm immobile, except for my eyes. Telecommunication has replaced the blood in my veins, forming a network across my flesh. I hear murmurs of activity race up and down my body. I'm attached to the ceiling—a human star with arms and legs outstretched like da Vinci's Vitruvian Man.

My eyes move from side to side, noticing others like me—their veins also glowing and buzzing. The ceiling is expanding, but we are going nowhere. The sound is getting louder. And we are becoming an unsettled symphony, waiting to short circuit at the drop of the virtual baton.

Frozen Kisses

Warmth has no home in a house built from ice—
love cannot express itself in any degree.
His lips are as frozen as mine
when we share our feelings by the windowsill.

Two trees watch our drama unfold behind glass,
see us as skeletons of themselves—
they stand bare and lifeless against the wind.

We pause to gaze out the window—
drawn to our reflections upon barren bark,
fully aware that our love is out of season.

Coming Home

If I came home,
would I find
our make-believe kids,
our nonexistent pets,
our thoughts,
our passion,
our past,
our lives,
ourselves?

But when I did,
no one
was at the stoop,
or entrance,
or in the hallway,
or by the kitchen table,
or near the bathroom sink,
or sitting on the sofa,
or resting on the bed,
or standing by the shade.

But your absence was everywhere;
it even took over the lease.

Open Space

Sunlight touches
the frames of two stories
where life dwelled and died.
Bricks built on love
were dismantled.
Hedges were evicted—
laughter and tears,
now homeless.
Ghosts of memories
roam a skeletal acre.
Greed buys it,
rebuilds in its image—
a reminder to others
that they might be next.

The Shabbat Eve

The sun exits
the auburn sky.
The lamb seasoned
for the ritual.
A miracle wrapped in a towel,
born from yeast, flour, and eggs.
Aromatherapy
dances around a table
set for one.

She covers her head
with her mother's scarf
made from Vilna's
tattered lace.
She covers her eyes
and prays over the candles.
She visualizes
what could have been
and wishes life were different.

An Ordinary Girl

She was an ordinary girl
who followed recipes
about marriage and kids.
She baked a cookie-cutter lifestyle
sprinkled with happiness.
She lived behind a picket fence,
away from certain dragons
out to destroy naïve girls.

But the dragons came early
and burned her recipes.
She grew up divorced
from sex.
Eggs fell off the shelves
inside her womb.
Her dream house crumbled,
and barbed wire replaced
the picket fence.

They rebuilt her house
with disillusion.
All doors and windows
were purposely omitted.
They stuffed her
with fantasies
from TV and magazines.
They recruited pawns
to checkmate her,
and she fell deeper
into the unreal.

Desperate for an exit,
she swallowed a few pills.
She took two more,
repeated this ritual
every half hour.

The walls around her
suddenly collapsed.
The foundation enlarged
to devour her,
but the dragons fell instead.
The nightmare ended,
but the girl never woke up.
She was found on the bathroom floor,
soaked in blood.

The Ghost

I'm the ghost
of days past, present,
and future—
an apparition
dressed in flesh and bone.
You've seen my past
and present—
you already know my future.

Your microscopic eyes
strip away secrets
beneath flesh and bone,
making me invisible—
never to claim my pain.

History happened,
and memories can't forget.
I may be a ghost,
but do the dead get resurrected?
Can the present cremate the past
to make peace with the future?
Can silence offer sanctuary
for what haunts your mind?
Can the imagination clothe
your secrets behind flesh and bone?

This ghost may never know.

When I Die

when I die,
    i don't want to see heaven or hell,
    or purgatory's waiting room.
    memories keep sending postcards
    so I won't forget heaven
    as the illusion
    that vaporized
    into the other two—
    the mirage
    that became quicksand below
    or the tornado above.

why did life's itinerary
    include these visits?
    why did oblivion
    get eliminated from this list?
    has anyone been to oblivion?
    is it a place
    where time forgot,
    where pain and joy ceased to exist,
    or where the cerebral hard drive crashed?

when i die,
    will i know
    if this is fact or fiction
    or will the truth vaporize
    when oxygen leaves my brain?

Small Dreams

We stand on the edge,
wait for elusive ships.
Small dreams grow into anxieties,
minutes tick away into hours,
hours clone themselves into days,
days into years,
and yesterday was tomorrow.

Our ostrich necks stretch,
see phantom ships.
Fog plays tag with hindsight,
clouds part
for reality to sail in.
We ask our watches for advice,
but time left for another port.

Scheduled Departures

Love has scheduled departures. And people purchase tickets, hoping to catch the next train out. It's always rush hour at this station. Lovers fill the corridors lined with shops and restaurants.

A feather sweeps by the entrance to Platform 9. I run past it. The stairwell leads me to where a train sits in temporary composure. After a few minutes, I see you boarding that train. You stand with your back turned. The doors close as your nonchalance faces your departure.

An hour passes. Another feather falls, but this time it lands in my hand. A train arrives on the opposite platform. The doors reopen. You leave the train and walk towards me. You say hello, handing me the feather you found by the entrance. But I never gave you mine. It fell to the tracks instead.

The Room

In the darkness, the room speaks another language—without traces of words or thought. Silence listens, then tries to translate, although the activity is too esoteric to be understood. Imagination would have done it, but it fell asleep in the adjacent room.

A child runs in and out of the rooms. She flicks the light switches on and off. Her laughter disturbs the peace. Imagination wakes up and leaves the adjacent room. It follows the child in a made-up song.

Silence returns to the darkness of the room, relieved that the song is fading downstairs. The room resumes its esoteric speech. Tranquility drops by. This time, the language is understood.

Unchaperoned

Some people try
to chaperone my life,
keep me within boundaries.
They're always right
and I'm always wrong.

Don't break the rules!
Shut up and dance!
You need to fit in!

I whirl past them,
tell them off.
Egos self-destruct—
their dogs break free
with tails wagging.

Mr. Lipson

Mr. Lipson,
you were a stone thrower,
paint tosser,
slasher,
arsonist.
You weren't Matisse,
van Gogh,
Rembrandt,
da Vinci,
or any great artist.
You were a cantankerous "old fart,"
a painter of "happy trees"
against mediocre landscapes.

You defaced two pieces of my artwork
in Aunt Celia's and Uncle Henry's
Stuyvesant Town living room,
as my parents sat
without intervening.

The pen-and-ink boat
capsized under faultfinding—
my lack of perspective,
my lack of experience.
Even the lighthouse couldn't be saved.

Your words deliberately smashed
the DayGlo pink bottle,
rotting the cheery flowers and fruit,
in and around the ceramic bowl—
too two-dimensional and amateurish.
Even the bowl cracked under pressure.

Not one word of encouragement
for an artist struggling
with pimples and self-worth—
an artist simultaneously
disappearing from her craft.

The pictures were intended for Aunt Celia—
she left space for them
to hang on the family art wall.
But instead,
they went into her closet.

A few years later,
Aunt Celia handed them back to me—
She said that they wouldn't fit in
with her collection,
but I saw that she made room for others.

I didn't argue—
instead,
I became a stone thrower,
paint tosser,
slasher,
arsonist.
I could never be Matisse,
van Gogh,
Rembrandt,
da Vinci,
or any great artist.
Nor could I become
a cantankerous "old bag,"
a painter of "happy trees"
against mediocre landscapes.
Remnants of the pen-and-ink boat and lighthouse,

and the DayGlo still life
were unceremoniously,
donated to the museum of garbage.

Years later,
I became a writer and poet.
But I'm not Dickinson,
Kerouac,
Bashō,
Woolf,
or any great writer or poet.
Just someone who writes
without paint or ink,
wondering ... *what would have happened
if Mr. Lipson read my work?*

Roller Coaster Train

We were approaching the last stop,
Coney Island—Stillwell Avenue,
but the N train didn't stop—

it continued upwards on tracks
that rose above the station
until it made that sudden descent

and plunged into the ocean
where the real mermaids waited
over an hour to get on.

The 4-Dimensional Man

The 4-dimensional man
contains 4 ideas,
4 times his squared root.

The 4-dimensional cat
contains more ideas,
but she's not telling.

Additional Acknowledgments

"Network." MÖBIUS, *The Poetry Magazine*, 30th Anniversary Issue, 2012.
"Frozen Kisses." First published in "The Ice Road Poems," *Fierce Grace Press*, 2007.
"Coming Home." First published in *Lips* Issue 34-35, April 2011.
"Open Space." *First Literary Review-East*, September 2012.
"The Shabbat Eve." First published in *Erato*, 2005.
"An Ordinary Girl." *Drunk Monkeys Poetry*, June 30, 2015.
"The Ghost." *Home Planet News Online*, Issue 1, April 2014.
"Small Dreams." First published in *Tamarind*, October 2012.
"Scheduled Departures." *Long Island Quarterly*, 2011.
"The Room," *MÖBIUS, The Poetry Magazine*, Vol. XXIII, 2008.
"Unchaperoned." *White Rabbit*, 2009.
"Mr. Lipson." *The Yellow Chair Review*, Issue 3, August 2015.
"Roller Coaster Train." First published in *Heavy Bear 3*, September 2009.
"4-Dimensional Man." First published in *Luciole Press*, 2008.

Brooklyn writer **Patricia Carragon** loves cupcakes, chocolate, cats, and haiku. Her publication credits include *Allbook Books, The Avocet, BigCityLit, Bear Creek Haiku, Boog City, CLWN WR, Clockwise Cat, Danse Macabre, Drunk Monkeys, Home Planet News, Inertia, Lips, Levure littéraire, Long Island Quarterly, Mad Hatters' Review, Maintenant, The Mom Egg, Panoply, poeticdiversity, Tribe Magazine, The Toronto Quarterly, Word Salad, Yellow Chair Review*, and others. She is the author of *Journey to the Center of My Mind* (Rogue Scholars Press, 2005) and *Urban Haiku and More* (Fierce Grace Press, 2010). *Cupcake Chronicles* is forthcoming from Poets Wear Prada. She hosts the Brooklyn-based Brownstone Poets and is the editor-in-chief of its annual anthology. Patricia is a member of brevitas, a group fiercely dedicated to short poems, and is a member of Pen Women's Literary Workshop and Tamarind. She is one of the Executive Editors for Home Planet News Online.

Patricia has featured at A Gathering of the Tribes, Bluestockings Bookstore, Bowery Poetry Club, Bright Hill Press, The Colony Arts Center, The Cornelia Street Café, the Green Pavilion, KGB Bar, Nuyorican Poets Café, the Poetry Barn, Robin's Bookstore, the Saturn Series, Sip This Café, Unnameable Books, and more.

For more information, please check out her websites:
http://brownstonepoets.blogspot.com/
https://patriciacarragon8.wordpress.com/

www.ingramcontent.com/pod-product-compliance
Lightning Source LLC
LaVergne TN
LVHW041601070426
835507LV00011B/1242